IMAGES
of America

CANYON LAKE

MAIN GATE ENTRANCE SIGN. This distinctive sign donated by the Lions Club appears at the main entrance to Canyon Lake. Its location at Railroad Canyon Road and Canyon Lake Drive South is visible to all vehicles driving from Sun City to Lake Elsinore. The logo for Canyon Lake, displayed at the end of the sign, has a waterfall flowing into the basin around the sign.

ON THE COVER: Appearing at the ribbon-cutting ceremony in April 1968 are, from left to right, Bill Jones (Riverside County supervisor, first district), Jeanette Bird (Miss Riverside County), Dino Serafini (vice president of Corona Land Company), and Donald Martin.

IMAGES
of America

CANYON LAKE

Elinor Martin

ARCADIA
PUBLISHING

Published by Arcadia Publishing
Charleston SC, Chicago IL, Portsmouth NH, San Francisco CA

Library of Congress Catalog Card Number 2006934433

For all general information contact Arcadia Publishing at:
Telephone 843-853-2070
Fax 843-853-0044
E-mail sales@arcadiapublishing.com
For customer service and orders:
Toll-Free 1-888-313-2665

Visit us on the Internet at www.arcadiapublishing.com

Dedicated to my parents, George Dewey and Leta Evans. My father loved this valley of his birth and my mother, being a teacher, recognized the importance of preserving the past through photographs for future generations.

CONTENTS

ACKNOWLEDGMENTS

I want to thank my husband, Donald Martin, for his patience and assistance with this project. Thank you to those persons who graciously answered my questions. The photographs in the book are from the Evans and Martin family personal collection, which has been amassed through the years. Temescal Water Company, Corona Land Company, and Gordon Heath generously added to our collection over 30 years ago. A special thanks to Sharon Johnson and Rhoda Wright for their assistance.

INTRODUCTION

Canyon Lake is a private, gated community located halfway between Lake Elsinore and Sun City, California. With a current population approaching 10,000 residents, this recreation-oriented community also has the distinction of being a fully governed city. In 1968, the Corona Land Company began construction on 5,000 lots around Railroad Canyon Lake. The pristine landscape—which had been virtually untouched since the 1890s, when there was only one family living and farming along the Salt Creek—dramatically changed and became one of Southern California's favorite playgrounds.

The San Jacinto River flows from the mountains east of Hemet, wanders through the valley down through Perris Valley, and finally ends at Lake Elsinore. When the winter rains arrive, Salt Creek follows a southern route from Hemet and merges with the San Jacinto at the location of present-day Canyon Lake.

The California Southern Railroad built a line in 1882 from Perris to Elsinore along the east side of the river. Later the Santa Fe Railroad bought the line and joined it with their line from San Bernardino. However, the floods of 1884, 1916, and 1927 washed out the tracks, and Santa Fe decided to abandon the line. Soon after the last flood, Temescal Water Company bought the railroad right-of-ways and began construction of a dam across the river for water storage.

In 1901, the Temescal Water Company of Corona spent $500,000 for the development of a water supply in Ethanac (now called Romoland) and its transportation through Railroad Canyon to Corona. Redwood pipes and open ditches carried the well water by gravity flow 40 miles to Corona. The company became embroiled in litigation over water rights for many years and, at one time, even owned Lake Elsinore but sold it in 1908 for $30,000. Around 1920, the water levels dropped in the Ethanac wells, and the water became saline and unusable. Plans were made to build a dam across the San Jacinto River for water storage. There were already open ditches and pipelines to continue the water flow to Corona, and Temescal Water obtained the land for the future reservoir by purchase or condemnation. Henry Evans, the largest landowner at that time, sold 1,150 acres to the company. Construction of the dam started in 1927 and was completed in 1929. A woman living below the construction site who objected to all the dust and noise would make barricades or stand in the road with a firearm and stop the truck traffic. The law took charge and forcibly removed her to a mental facility for observation. Upon her release, she returned, burned her house down, and willed the property to the president of the United States.

Joy Jamison, then president of the Temescal Water Company, became the brunt of "Jamison's folly" jokes made by board members in Corona when, after the completion of the dam, sparse rains prevented the river from bringing water. Eventually winter rains returned, and the lake slowly began to fill with water. A tunnel being drilled in the San Jacinto Mountains sent nice freshwater down the river, as well as fish from ponds along its course, which continued to reproduce in the new lake. After a few years, the water company considered leasing the area as a concession for public fishing. In the meantime, George Evans, the son of original landowner Henry Evans, was leasing land from Temescal for cattle grazing. George and Leta Evans were granted the concession rights, and a business friendship that would last 30 years started. Even the Evanses' three daughters and their husbands—Ray and Alpha Schekel, John and Darleen Kirkland, and Donald and Elinor Martin (the author)—would take turns running the fishing business.

The business started in 1937 when the Evans family built a small concession stand, bought several boats and food supplies, and opened to customers on May 29. They did not expect such instant success, but the narrow two-lane road would often be backed up for miles with carloads of eager fishermen. Word had spread quickly about the new lake and its great fishing, though local anglers had known about it for several years. George cut his pasture fences so customers could reach the lake more easily. The Evans Fish Camp grew, and several years later, its buildings and docks were moved farther west to another location on the lake, where the water remained deep, even in drought years.

After World War II, Ray and Alpha Schekel, along with John and Darleen Kirkland, operated the resort until 1949, when the lake was drained to repair the floodgates on the dam. Winter rains came once again, and the lake slowly filled with water. In 1951, the Department of Fish and Game restocked the lake, and the heavy rains of 1952 brought the water level high enough that the resort could reopen in 1953. The author and her husband, Donald, then operated the resort until 1968.

Elsinore Valley Municipal Water District and Temescal Water Company reached a settlement in 1955 to store 3,000 acre-feet of water in the lake for domestic use. A treatment plant was erected, and later fish screens were installed over the floodgates so that all the fish would not travel downstream to Lake Elsinore. After the collapse of the Baldwin Hills Dam in 1963, the state ordered all dams inspected and reinforced. Cores were taken, and the concrete was found to be stronger than current requirements.

February 1968 saw the beginning of a new era. Temescal bought the lease from the Evans family, and the development of Canyon Lake began. Several subsidiary companies were formed from the original Temescal Water Company, and eventually Corona Land Company became the developer of the project.

Today the lake is surrounded by beautiful homes, and residents enjoy many amenities, such as a golf course, equestrian center, beaches, parks, and a lodge. The Canyon Lake Property Owners Association has jurisdiction inside the gates, and property owners pay a yearly assessment. In December 1990, the community became a city, and all of the areas outside the gates are under the jurisdiction of the city council.

The original developers had envisioned a weekend-retreat type of community, but current residents include retirees, young families, and those looking for security or a change of residence. The areas surrounding Canyon Lake are rapidly becoming urban. The purpose of this book is to illustrate the community's history and its visual changes recorded by photographic images taken during the last 100 years.

One

THE EARLY YEARS
1890 to 1936

THOMAS JEFFERSON EVANS (1826–1901). Thomas Evans was born in Indiana, came to California during the gold rush, and settled in San Bernardino in 1875. His son Henry moved to Menifee in 1890, and the next year, his father bought the property for him. Thomas's journal states, "I swapped house and lot on corner of H and 10th street (San Bernardino) to M. Easton with $250 note for their 100 acre farm where Henry lives." The 100-acre farm was the homestead at the east end of Canyon Lake, located near Newport and Railroad Canyon Roads.

HENRY HARTLEY EVANS (1863–1930).
Henry Evans came to San Bernardino with his parents in 1875, married Ella Ferrell, and moved to Menifee Valley in 1890. This area is now Canyon Lake. His in-laws arrived three years earlier and lived on what is now the Audie Murphy ranch. Farming was his occupation, and in 1915, he became district-road foreman for Menifee. In 1927, he sold his property (1,150 acres) to the Temescal Water Company.

GEORGE DEWEY AND LETA EVANS, 1919. Pictured here are George Dewey and Leta Evans on their wedding day in 1919. George was born in 1897 on the family ranch in Menifee. He farmed, and Leta taught school in Menifee and Temecula. They later moved a house from Coop Station to Antelope Road, where they raised three daughters and spent half of each year at Railroad Canyon Lake, operating the fishing resort from 1937 to 1967.

EVANS RANCH, THEN AND NOW. This photograph shows the ranch of Henry and Ella Evans in 1910. Their son Fred is standing in the foreground by his apiary. A chuckwagon is parked beside the house, and a horse and wagon is picking up hay in the field. Henry never turned a man away who came to his door. Hobos were always welcome to a meal, and they left marks on fence posts nearby so others would know it was a good place for a meal or some work. The present-day location would be at the north end of White Wake Drive. The photograph below shows the same view as it looks today. The open land is along Goetz Road on the way to Quail Valley.

HENRY AND ELLA EVANS. Henry and Ella Evans are ready to go visiting in their horse-and-buggy. This was the transportation available in the early days. Perris, Elsinore, and Winchester were the nearest towns for supplies. The *Perris Progress* reported that Henry put in his order for a 1916 four-door Ford and was later seen driving it around the valley and showing it to his friends.

PICNIC ALONG THE RIVER. The William Brown family is shown here enjoying a picnic along the San Jacinto River at Railroad Canyon on March 18, 1917. It was common for Menifee Valley residents to gather and enjoy outings along the river and in Cottonwood Canyon. (Courtesy Rosamond Morrison.)

Santa Fé Railway Station, Perris, Cal.

PERRIS SANTA FE DEPOT. The California Southern Railroad built a line from Perris to Elsinore in 1882. Its location through the canyon was on the east side of the San Jacinto River. The first station was at Pinacate, now the location of the Orange Empire Railway Museum. After a title dispute over the land in 1886, the station was moved about a mile and half north to Perris. Pictured here is the original depot, built in 1892. The building is now the home of the Perris Valley Historical and Museum Association. The railroad line was later sold to the Santa Fe Railroad and became part of its transcontinental line. The 1910 postcard below looks north down Main Street in Elsinore.

MAIN ST.
ELSINORE, CAL.

1910

FLOOD OF 1927. These pictures show the damage caused by the flood of February 16, 1927. The bridge washed out from under the tracks at the southern end, where the current freeway meets Railroad Canyon Road. In the narrow canyon north of the bridge, the force of the water ripped the tracks from their bed. The damage was great—this was the third washout the railroad had experienced since 1882, and the decision was made to abandon the line. (Courtesy Loretta Eckes and E. Hale Curran).

GUARDING THE HERD. The train tracks curved before arriving at the section house in Railroad Canyon. Visibility was limited, and it was the duty of the Evans boys to make sure no cows, which liked to lie on the warm tracks, were on them when the train from Perris was due. Note the telegraph lines along the track. The current location is just north of Big Bass Cove.

ANNUAL CATTLE ROUNDUP. In later years, George Evans pastured cattle and hosted an annual barbecue for the cattle owners. The event was held on a wooded area at the north end of Railroad Canyon called Armentrout. A stream coming into the lake furnished fresh water, and a small pond was available for swimming. The entire Menifee Valley was invited, and all had a good time.

REDWOOD WATER PIPELINES. Temescal Water Company of Corona purchased 2,560 acres in Ethanac (now Romoland) near Perris for a water source in 1901. It drilled wells and transported the water in various types of pipelines to company groves in Temescal Canyon and Corona. Pictured here are pipes built of redwood, with steel bands holding the 36-inch wood staves together. The pipes had a concrete casing for protection from the elements. The line followed the west side of the San Jacinto River down to Elsinore and joined other lines. The Evans family would use this salvaged redwood for years to come.

DIFFERENT PIPELINE VIEWS. These two photographs show more details about the pipeline coming from Ethanac. Sixteen wells were drilled at Ethanac, and 40 miles of pipeline was needed to transport the water to its destination in Corona. The Temescal Water Company faced litigation for many years over water rights. About 1920, the water level dropped and the wells became too saline to use. The company was planning a storage reservoir in the San Jacinto River, and after the Santa Fe Railroad abandoned their line in 1927, Temescal Water bought their right-of-way.

RAILROAD CANYON DAM CONSTRUCTION. Construction of the dam started in 1927, after Temescal condemned or purchased the necessary lands. The project faced opposition from the citizens in Elsinore, and eventually an agreement known as the Tilly Agreement was reached and construction continued. A woman living below the dam physically opposed the project, and after reaching a settlement with the company, she burned her house and willed the property to the president of the United States.

RAILROAD CANYON DAM. The dam across the San Jacinto River was completed in 1929. Financing was available from the sale of the Ethanac lands. Dry winters followed the completion of the dam, and the resulting empty reservoir became a source of amusement among the Temescal Water Company's board members. They called it "Jamison's folly" after Joy Jamison, then president of the company. Later the reservoir became a lifeline for Temescal Canyon.

COTTONWOOD CANYON BRIDGE. Pictured here is the Cottonwood Canyon Bridge, located below the dam. The burned remains of a house show in the foreground. Riverside County built the bridge in 1917 at a cost of $18,000. Henry Evans was supervisor of the project and kept a journal of the expenses. Current landmarks place the old road from Menifee to Elsinore as follows: Newport Road to White Wake Drive, across Salt Creek (now East Bay) to Continental Drive, south to the golf course, turn right and follow the creek to the bridge (shown in the photograph), cross the bridge, and continue along the west side of the river to a crossing near Summerhill Drive and into Elsinore on the existing roads. The roads were two-lane dirt, and the mile beyond the bridge was narrow and curvy. A new road built in August 1949 follows the existing Railroad Canyon Road.

SCHOOL FRIENDS, MAY 31, 1931. Pictured here from left to right and submerged are Ida May Bailey, Grace Crawford, Alice Roberts, Miss McFarland (teacher at Antelope School), Gladys Bailey, and Darleen Evans. Pictured standing are Alpha Evans (pointing), unidentified, and Alpha's mother, Leta Evans (wearing hat). Another unidentified woman stands on the shoreline. They are in the San Jacinto River near the current Big Bass Cove.

FRANK SWANSON HOUSE. The house pictured here was the residence of Arthur and Frank Swanson. The two bachelors moved into the house about 1924 and lived there until their deaths. Corona Land Company purchased their land shortly before Frank's death. It was located among the sycamore trees at the No. 11 tee, at the south end of the country club's parking lot. (Courtesy Robert Wickerd.)

Two

PUBLIC FISHING RESORT
1937 TO 1967

FIRST EVANS FISH CAMP. George and Leta Evans received a lease from the Temescal Water Company in 1937 to operate a concession at Railroad Canyon Lake. Fishing permits, bait, pop, and candy were available at this structure, located at the east end of the lake (now called Indian Beach). The family bought a few cases of soda pop and some candy, and used a box as their cash register. Standing on the step is their daughter Darleen. George was born on the ranch just east of Indian Beach and spent his early years working and herding cattle on the land that is now covered with water, then moved to Antelope Road after his marriage. His occupation prior to 1937 was raising hogs and pasturing cattle on the land his father once owned.

CONCESSION STAND REST AREA. The area behind the concession stand provided the family a place to rest. Fishing hours were about a half hour before sunrise to about a half hour after sunset. The anglers liked an early start, so that made a long day for the family. Leta Evans stands on the right, and daughter Alpha lies on the bed. The little girl is unidentified.

EARLY POSTCARD. This early postcard shows two unidentified men holding a string of largemouth bass. Ten bass a day was the limit, and they had to be at least nine inches long. The word spread about the great fishing and crowds arrived. George Evans lived by the belief that if an angler arose early and drove 80 miles to give him his money, he could get up early and accept it.

FISHING BOATS FOR RENT. The Evans Fish Camp had a few boats of different styles that were available for rent. They were an odd-looking fleet but served their purpose. Because no dock was available that first year, they tied the boats to the trees or pulled them up on the shore.

ELLA EVANS IN A BOAT. Pictured here is Ella Evans, mother of George Evans, sitting in one of the boats. Ella and her husband, Henry, owned this property from 1890 to 1927, when Temescal Water Company bought the land for the reservoir. Ella's grandchildren said she had many memories of this area before the lake covered the land with water.

OPENING DAY, MAY 1937. The lake opened to the public for the first time in 1937, but word already had spread about the great fishing. It seems that a few people had previously sampled the waters. A tunnel was built in the San Jacinto Mountains, and freshwater flowed down the San Jacinto River, bringing fish from the ponds along the way. The Evanses did not expect this large of a crowd and were not prepared. Automobiles backed up so far that George had to cut the fences of his pasture to allow vehicles to enter the area. Many customers set up camp for the weekend.

TYPICAL WEEKEND SCENE. The top photograph shows the cars parking along the flat shoreline. The eucalyptus trees on the right still exist and are part of the Indian Beach Park area. The hills in the background are located in the present-day Quail Valley. Anglers drove around the lake to find a less crowded spot if they did not have a boat. A boat dock was built to accommodate anglers. The open space on the far side of the lake once grew wheat and was farmed by Henry Evans.

WEEKDAYS AT EVANS FISH CAMP. Attendance slowed during the weekdays, and the Evanses worked on enlarging the facilities to accommodate the large weekend crowds. Quite a few customers were able to enjoy the solitude during the week before the weekend crowds arrived.

PRIMITIVE CAMPGROUND, 1938. There were no designated campsites on the grounds of the first fish camp. Customers pitched their tents on any available space that appealed to them. There were no fancy camping vehicles in those days. Shade was at a premium, and areas that had it were quickly claimed by the first to arrive. The trees still are growing at Indian Beach.

DIFFERENT VIEW OF THE AREA. This photograph shows the area from the north side of the lake looking south. Indian Beach would be on the left, and where the cars are parking would now be Gray Fox Drive. The tallest hill is behind the present-day Fairway Estates and is part of the Canyon Hills subdivision.

RENTAL BOATS AND DOCK. This photograph shows the dock and rental boats. A pair of oars manually propelled the heavy wooden boats unless one provided his own outboard motor. Some customers used their own boats. The high mountain in the middle of the picture is located in Quail Valley before Goetz Road turns toward Perris.

NEW OFFICE BUILDING. Expansion became necessary, and a building was erected for conducting business and for use as living quarters for the family. It became the Evans family home for six months each year. Temescal Water Company's abandoned pipeline furnished redwood lumber for the porch. The building, later moved to a different location, was razed 30 years later in 1968 to make way for the Village Store in Canyon Lake.

CABINS AND OUTBUILDINGS. Improvements continued and several cabins were erected to house employees. Paid employees included a cook, waitress, boatman, and handyman. Relatives all pitched in to help on busy holidays. The windows were screened openings with a wooden flap for colder days. Air conditioning was not an option in any of the buildings. Isinglass on the flaps allowed light to filter into the buildings.

OVERFLOWING OF RAILROAD CANYON DAM. This 1938 postcard shows the dam overflowing after heavy rains. The catwalk above the dam gave the caretaker access to the machinery that opened and closed the floodgates at the base of the dam. Standing on the catwalk when the dam overflowed was an awesome experience remembered by the author. Gus Johnson was the caretaker for many years.

ANGLER AND LARGEMOUTH BASS. Pictured here is Walter Graham of San Pedro, holding about a five-pound bass and some smaller ones. Many anglers preferred using fly rods. Lures for casting rods included such colorful names as injured minnow, flatfish, dingbat, crazy crawler, and river runts. Today these lures are collectibles and are very pricey.

LIMIT OF LARGEMOUTH BASS. Seen here are Mr. and Mrs. Cleveland with their limit of bass, totaling 15 pounds. They set up camp, fished, and enjoyed themselves during the weekends and became loyal customers for many years. The author remembers customers that came regularly and seemed like part of the family.

ANGLERS AND THEIR CATCHES. Having reached the limit, Larry Evans (left) and his friend show off their bass. Evans lived in San Bernardino, was a regular customer, and came several times a week but was not related to the family. His special raised chair made fly fishing easier. Space was at a premium in the boat after one loaded all the fishing gear.

ANOTHER VIEW OF BOAT DOCK. This early dock floated on old telephone poles that formed a type of raft. Boat rentals were $1.50 a day, and fishing permits cost 50¢ a person. In the 1950s, the rates increased to $3 for boats and permits to $1. Neptune outboard motors became available for rent in 1938. This photograph looks directly east from the current Indian Beach.

GAME WARDENS. Wardens from the Fish and Game Department patrolled the lake almost every weekend. One in particular was Jim Gyger of Perris, who was a strict and by-the-book sort of man. Harriet, his wife, always remembered the birthdays of the Evans women and presented them with personalized handmade handkerchiefs.

NEW FISH CAMP SITE, 1940. When the water level started receding, the decision was made to move the buildings and docks to a deeper part of the lake. The buildings were levered onto large skids and towed with tractors to their new location. (The current location would be on Village Way.) This photograph shows the crowd on opening day in May 1940. Opening days were usually set for the last weekend in May.

DOCKS IN OFF-SEASON. During the off-season, boats were drydocked and repaired. This scene shows the boats at the new location, ready for repair. Cracks were sealed, and a new coat of paint was applied for the coming season. The point of land at the top of the photograph is the location of the present-day lodge.

ANGLERS SHOWING OFF CATCHES. The lake level in 1941 was high and fishing was great. These unidentified anglers show off the largemouth bass they caught before packing up their gear to return home. The lake was one of the best bass-fishing lakes in Southern California.

NEW DESIGNATED CAMPGROUND. Cabana-type shades provided the campers with protection from the summer heat. Roofs were made of wire mesh covered in palm fronds, which were replaced each season. It is amazing no fires ever occurred when the leaves dried in the heat. Each campsite was equipped with a stove made from a used 300-pound ice-block mold, with a round hole for the smoke to escape.

POSTCARD OF THE LAKE. This postcard shows the area about 1942. The large building on the left was a picnic room for customers. Alpha, the oldest Evans daughter, held her wedding reception there in 1940. George Evans allowed only two families to build cabins for their personal use, and Harry Divine, a regular customer, built the large cabin in the foreground.

FLOODGATES, BASE OF DAM. Water was released through two floodgates at the base of the dam. Lake Elsinore was entitled to a portion of the water that flowed from Salt Creek each year. The lengthy Tilley Agreement settled a dispute in October 1927 between Temescal Water Company and other interested parties. The agreement detailed the distribution of water from Salt Creek.

RAILROAD CANYON LAKE
Phone Elsinore
MAIN 2173

THIRTY MILES OF SHORELINE

Crappie, Bass and Blue Gill Fishing

Duck Hunting

Boats and Motors   Lunch Room

GEO. D. EVANS   Romoland, Rt. 1, California

[OVER]

EARLY BUSINESS CARD. This early business card reflects the rural nature of the address and phone number. If one drove from Elsinore to Railroad Canyon Lake before 1949, the entrance would appear on the north side of the road after crossing the bridge just below the dam.

The dirt road traversed a steep hill until it reached the area that is now the end of Sparkle Drive. The realignment of Railroad Canyon Road in 1949 moved it to the east side of the river and followed the route of the current road. George Evans built a new entrance to the lake, which was at the location of the existing main gate. Interstate 215 eventually replaced the freeway known as Highway 395.

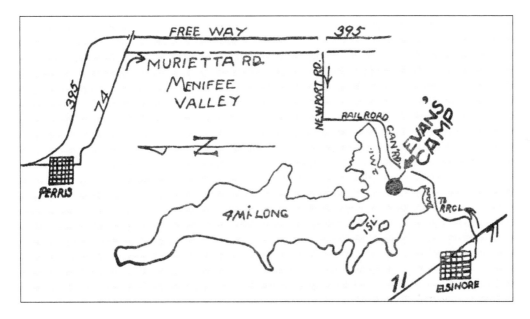

RAILROAD CANYON LAKE

RIVERSIDE COUNTY NEAR ELSINORE OR PERRIS

Eighty Miles from Los Angeles - Eighty Miles north of San Diego

Fishing and Hunting

FISHING SEASON OPENS

FISHING PERMITS $1.00 Per Day   50 BOATS $2 Per Day   MOTORS 4$ Per Day

Boats should be reserved for Holidays and week ends.   -   All boats not called
for by 7:00 a. m., will be cancelled unless boat and permits paid for in advance.
No Motors over 7½ H. P. or Inboards Allowed.
Open Every Day from April 15th to close of Fishing Season.

Write: **GEORGE D. EVANS**

RT. 1, ROMOLAND   PHONE ELSINORE MAIN 2173

CAMP GROUNDS - STORE - LUNCH COUNTER - TACKLE - WORMS

ANNUAL ADVERTISING PLACARD. These small, six-by-eight-inch advertising posters were mailed to all sporting-goods stores in Southern California to be displayed in windows. Weekly fishing reports also went out to all the interested newspapers, and several sports writers phoned Sunday night for fishing reports. A mailing list compiled from the fishing permits advised customers as to the date of the next year's opening day.

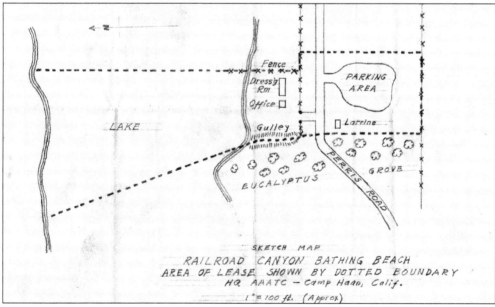

MILITARY AQUATIC CENTER MAP. This map details the area the military leased for training soldiers at Indian Beach. About 1944, the army leased the site to train soldiers in water exercises. They were required to jump from a tower carrying a full backpack and to swim to shore. Other troops from Camp Haan often staged war games around the lake.

EVANS FAMILY IN 1940 AND 1946. The top photograph shows the family about 1940. Pictured here are, from left to right, the following: (first row) Leta and George; (second row) Alpha, the author, and Darleen. The bottom photograph is from around 1946. Standing behind the display case from left to right are John and Darleen Kirkland, Alpha and Ray Schekel (back), George and Leta Evans, Minnie and Darrell King, and the author, holding nephew David Kirkland. Customers could buy fishing and camping permits, rent boats, and purchase bait and tackle here. Three generations of the Evans family worked behind this counter.

RAYMOND SCHEKEL, C. 1947. Raymond Schekel shows off a catch of bass while standing beside the company pickup. Raymond and Alpha Schekel and John and Darleen Kirkland operated the resort from 1946 until about 1950, when the lake closed. Alpha and Darleen were the daughters of George and Leta Evans. George and Leta Evans semiretired after their sons-in-law returned from military service.

RAILROAD CANYON DAM REPAIR. Temescal Water Company needed to repair the floodgates of the dam, so they drained the lake in 1949. Water was released into Lake Elsinore, and fish were relocated to other lakes. This photograph shows the floodgates at the bottom of the dam and water backed up at a level lower than the gates.

WATER BEHIND THE DAM. This small pond of water was below the floodgate level and did not drain. The view looks north from the dam, and the campground of today would be on the left side. This occurred in 1949, and the resort was closed. The Schekel and Kirkland families left the area to pursue other occupations.

DRY LAKE BED. The draining of the lake left the resort high and dry. This photograph shows the lake bottom exposed. The island is on the left and the point (or current lodge site) on the right. It was exciting to discover all the old fishing lures and unusual items that were lost when the lake was full.

EAST BAY VIEW. The cattle shown here are grazing in the dry lake bottom. The trees on the right show the current location of Indian Beach. The present-day Gray Fox Drive would be on the right edge of the photograph. Often the lake was narrow at this point and the cattle could easily swim across it. A motorboat discouraged them during the roundup, when they were reluctant to go to the barn area.

DONALD MARTIN AND CATTLE. The cattle needed extra feed during the years with dry winters. Donald Martin, pictured here, has just finished unloading hay and is standing in the location of today's Mariners Bay. After loading the truck with bales of hay, Martin would drive along honking the horn, and the cattle would come running. The author, who is Martin's wife, or son Stephen would drive while he tossed them hay.

40

WHITEFACE HEREFORD CATTLE. This herd of whiteface Herefords waits by the fence to enter the next pasture. Their location today would be at the intersection of Canyon Lake Drive North and Vacation Drive. The Evans family kept a herd of about 300 cattle for over 20 years, until Canyon Lake began. The cattle grazed on the 3,000 acres of leased or owned land surrounding the lake.

RED CATTLE BARN. This barn, built in 1947, was used in the cattle operation. The middle section provided storage for hay bales, and the side sections were equipped with mangers to feed any livestock kept inside. The annual roundup brought the herd to the barn, and the calves were separated from their mothers. Calves weighing 300 to 400 pounds went to the livestock market in Los Angeles.

CAMPGROUNDS IN 1954. The lake reopened April 15, 1953, after the heavy winter rains of 1952. The restocking of the fish population occurred in 1951. The author worked at the resort, while her husband, Donald, was serving in the army and was stationed in Korea. After his discharge from the military in 1954, the couple, along with Leta Evans, continued to operate the resort until 1968. They leveled new pads for additional campsites, built more cabanas—covering them with redwood lumber instead of palm fronds to reduce the fire hazard—and replaced the roofs of the older cabanas. Several years later, a modern trailer park with full hookups was completed and made available to the public.

SNOW STORM, 1957. The morning of January 29, 1957, brought a surprise to the area. Seen here is Donald Martin standing by his pickup. Heavy snowfall was unusual. According to several Elsinore historians, snow fell in that valley in 1896, 1916, 1932, and 1949.

BOATS READY FOR REPAIR. The boats pictured here await repairs for the coming season. The estimated depth of the snowfall was five to six inches, according to the pileup on the boat bottoms. During the winter, a Fordson tractor equipped with a forklift on the bucket brought the boats to the parking lot for repairs.

DAMAGE TO CAMPGROUND CABANAS. This photograph shows some of the damage to the campground cabanas. The weight of the snow caused these two to break and fall on a truck parked underneath. The site pictured here would be on the current Holiday Harbor and along Village Way. Considering the amount of snowfall, there was very little damage.

NORTH VIEW OF THE LAKE. This view of the lake, taken from the camping area, shows the shorelines covered with snow. The island appears on the left of the photograph, and on the right side is the area now occupied by Sunset Beach and the lodge. The thin strip of white in between the two was once the old railroad bed.

SNOW DAMAGE TO TREES. The weight of the snow caused considerable damage to the trees, but most of them survived. The snow hampered work for a few days but quickly melted, and life went on as usual. The Martin family was busy taking photographs to document this unusual occurrence.

RAILROAD CANYON LAKE ENTRANCE. This photograph shows the Martins' 1954 Crown Victoria Ford parked at the main gate. They were returning from checking out the snowfall in the surrounding communities. The author remembered the large snowfall of 1949 in Menifee and wanted to take photographs of her home place, 10 miles east, but after arriving, she was disappointed to find only a light dusting of snow.

GOETZ ROAD CROSSING. Marvin Brewer, manager of Temescal Water Company, checks the water flow over Goetz Road near Perris. A bridge now spans this crossing. Elsinore Valley Municipal Water District reached an agreement with Temescal in November 1955 for 3,000 acre-feet of water storage for domestic use. The imported Colorado River water left a pipeline in Lakeview, and gravity flow brought it down the San Jacinto River to the lake. The water district built a treatment plant near the dam, and the lake became a domestic water supply. Signs and plaques posted in the boats warned of any bodily contact, and swimming and wading no longer were an option. Later the use of a different method of treating the water allowed for swimming and other recreational activities.

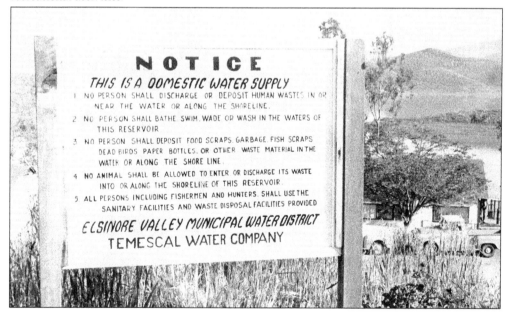

DUCK AND GOOSE HUNTING.
Standing beside the gasoline pump
are the author and her husband,
Donald Martin. The lake opened for
hunting on Wednesdays, Saturdays,
and Sundays during the season.
Donald enjoyed hunting, and he
proudly displayed these Canadian
geese and ducks. As the sign states,
the cost of a full day of hunting was
$2. Dove-and rabbit-hunting season
usually started September 1, and the
duck season in November. Temescal
Water Company wanted the lake for
a private hunting club, and for several
years, it was closed to the public.
The group pictured below are, from
left to right, as follows: (first row)
unidentified, Marvin Brewer, George
Graham, Harry House, and Crawford
Teague; (second row) Ted Todd,
Jim Morris, G. Christensen, Doctor
Johnson, and Donald Martin.

BOAT DOCK AND RENTAL BOATS. These photographs were taken in 1967 on the south side of the lake directly across from the current lodge. A fleet of 100 new wooden boats occupied two docks and usually sold out on the weekends. Reservations were available and held until 7:00 a.m., and 40 Mercury outboard motors were available for rent. A boat and motor rented for $8 the entire day. There was a full-time boatman, and on weekends, high school age boys from Perris cleaned and mopped the boats for the next morning. Bruce Cowie, one of those boys, recently told the author it was the best job he ever had during his high school years.

DISPLAY OF LARGEMOUTH BASS. Standing behind the showcase counter, Donald Martin shows off three largemouth bass. Large fish were often displayed in an ice chest with a glass cover, so the unlucky fisherman could see what got away. Cards of spinner-type lures cover the back wall, and the showcase displays all types of fishing lures and other supplies.

MIKE AND LOYD FOLKESTAD, 1955. Mike (left) and his father, Loyd, display their catch of largemouth bass. This duo from Long Beach loved to fish and were regular customers. Mike became successful on the professional bass circuit in later years. He recalls coming to Railroad Canyon Lake as a teenager, sleeping on a table in the campground, and cleaning boats in exchange for the use of one.

NEW TRAILER PARK. Construction of a modern trailer park with complete hookups accommodated the growing number of campers who preferred facilities that were more convenient. This photograph shows its location above Village Way. The point of land on the right is the location of Sunset Beach and the current lodge, while Treasure Island appears on the left.

OVERFLOW DRY CAMPING. Busy weekends and holidays found campers parking on any level space available. This overflow area would now be near Holiday Harbor on Village Way. The lake area was a popular destination for camping clubs from Orange County. The hills in the background are now part of Tuscany Hills and are covered with homes.

RAILROAD CANYON RESERVOIR. In this postal card, anglers are fishing at the log boom near the dam. Boats or fisherman are prohibited from trespassing closer to the dam. In the years after Canyon Lake became a reality, the walkway was removed and the sides of the dam cut back to allow floodwaters to flow from the lake more easily.

RAILROAD CANYON LAKE RESORT. This postcard shows the resort area on the south shore of the lake across from the current lodge. Fishing, boating, and camping facilities were available to the public from May to November. Several homes, Holiday Harbor, and the boat-launch ramp now occupy this location.

RAILROAD CANYON LAKE RESORT
ROMOLAND, CALIFORNIA (RIVERSIDE COUNTY)

AERIAL VIEW OF LAKE. This postcard gives an aerial view of Canyon Lake. Treasure Island appears on the left, and the current lodge site is on the right. The main road to the resort appears in the foreground, and the trailer park is in the middle. A photograph taken today would show houses side by side around the shoreline.

POSTCARD OF FISHING ACTIVITY. Two anglers holding their limit of bass stand in their boat. The building at the top of the photograph is the office and café. The café served a limited menu for breakfast and lunch and sold a few groceries and block ice.

VILLAGE WAY, THEN AND NOW. The top photograph shows the area as it looked in the early 1960s on a busy weekend, with anglers fishing from the shoreline. The home of the author and her husband, Donald, appears at the top of the photograph. The bottom photograph is the same location in 2006. Looking south across the lake from the lodge on Canyon Club Drive, Holiday Harbor and many homes can be seen where the resort was once located. The Martin home remains in the same location, now surrounded by new homes, but has a new address and is not as visible as it is in the top photograph.

ANOTHER VIEW OF THE RESORT. This 1958 photograph shows a view of the resort from the area where the main causeway met the north shore. The causeway of today would begin in the left foreground of the photograph, go south across the lake, and end near the little cove on the left, where several cars are parked.

QUIET DAY AT THE LAKE. Quiet weekdays at the lake prompted several amateur poets to write poems about it. During the early 1940s, a few film stars also enjoyed the lake. Some of the regular customers became like family and even pitched in to help if there was an emergency.

30TH ANNIVERSARY CELEBRATION, 1967. Evans Fish Camp opened May 29, 1937, and 30 years later, in June 1967, celebrated its 30th anniversary with a party and fishing contest for its customers. Memories of those years were the topic of the day among family and friends. Pictured above are, from left to right, hosts Belle McGrath, the author, Mildred Martin, and Leta Evans serving refreshments. Winners of the fishing contest pictured at right are E. Crocker and J. Ortiz, with Greg Millar (right) handing out the prizes. The first-place winner received a Mercury outboard motor, and the second-place winner got a tackle box and lures.

THE END OF AN ERA. The demolition in 1968 of the building that housed the resort office and café signaled the end of an era. It was built in 1938, a year after the first fish camp opened at the east end of the lake, and was moved to this location, where it remained for the next 28 years. The porch, constructed of redwood lumber from the pipeline that Temescal Water Company used to transport water from Ethanac to Corona in 1901, received a new coat of gray paint annually. Three generations of the Evans family occupied the living quarters in the rear of the building. The author had tears in her eyes upon seeing the building being reduced to a pile of lumber and going up in smoke.

Three

BEGINNING A NEW ERA
1968 TO PRESENT

RIBBON-CUTTING CEREMONY, APRIL 1968.
February 1968 saw the beginning of a new era
for the lake known as Railroad Canyon. The
lake would become a private recreational area
surrounded with homes and used exclusively
by homeowners and their guests. Its gated
entrances would ensure security for the
residents. Gordon Heath, Foothill Lemon
Company, and Temescal Water Company of
Corona started the development planning in
1967. Heath had previously worked for five
years for the Del Webb Company in Sun City
and had visualized a community around the
lake. He would rent a boat, take a briefcase,
and spend hours on the lake with no fishing
gear. He revealed later that he was laying out
the master plan. A settlement with the Evans
and Martin family was finalized February
12, 1968, and construction began. Standing
on the corner of Canyon Lake Drive South
and Village Way for this April 1968 publicity
photograph are, from left to right, Bill Jones
(Riverside County supervisor, first district),
Jeanette Bird (Miss Riverside County), Dino
Serafini, (vice president of Corona Land
Company), and Donald Martin.

CONSTRUCTION TO BEGIN. Lined up in rows and ready to work are bulldozers and earth-moving equipment. Since a main-entrance road already was in place, the equipment started on the causeway and moved to the north side of the east-bay area, raising that shoreline higher to accommodate more building pads. The south side of the bay from the causeway to Indian Beach remained natural terrain, but east of Indian Beach, the shoreline changed dramatically. The shoreline around the rest of the lake remained natural terrain with a few exceptions here and there.

CHANGES IN THE NATURAL TERRAIN. A newspaper article in 1968 stated, "Canyon Lake will be a 45 million dollar subdivision recreational development of 2,017 acres, in approximately three square miles. The reservoir will be expanded and shoreline lengthened by dredging and filling along the fingers of land, moving approximately 2.5 million cubic feet of dirt." This photograph shows the area around Canyon Lake Drive North under construction.

ORIGINAL ENTRANCE TO THE LAKE. This original entrance is the first road visitors would see upon arriving to tour the new development. Now named Canyon Lake Drive South, it is still the main thoroughfare. The first two tracts opened for sale appeared along this road and quickly sold.

BUILDING THE ENTRANCE. All phases of construction were happening at the same time, but an impressive entrance was one of the first priorities. Construction began on a huge waterfall, bridge, and pond. The water cascaded 18 feet into a 5,000-square-foot pond. Jim Carter was the first to drive a car across the oak-plank bridge, on March 23, 1968. The loose planks made a clattering noise when a vehicle crossed them, giving the sensation of an old-fashioned bridge. A few imported ducks made their home in the pond. Later this waterfall on the northwest corner of Canyon Lake Drive South and Continental Drive was leveled and sold as a building site.

WATERFALL AND NEW ENTRANCE SIGN. Initially visitors would arrive via a two-lane road from Elsinore and the Sun City area. The four-lane road through the project was not built until later. A new sign at the entrance would direct people into the project. After turning off Railroad Canyon Road, visitors would continue over the bridge and meet a security person, who would direct them to the sales office. At this particular time, no official guard gate existed, and the main road was unpaved. Looking around the entrance area today, it is hard to believe that only a few small juniper trees once adorned that area.

MAIN ROAD, LOOKING WEST. The eucalyptus trees on the left were planted in the 1950s, and few remain today. While the building sites were under construction, utilities were being installed underground. The workers encountered at least three different types of soil in this first mile of road. This new method for laying curbs—by extrusion—was quickly switched to the regular method—using forms—due to the rough terrain.

DISPLAY BOOTH AT THE FAIR. While the community was being built, a sales force was busy reaching out to customers. This display booth at the Los Angeles County Fair gave information to interested persons. Articles about the project appeared in most Southern California papers, and a direct-mail program was in progress. The new private community surrounding a lake was generating a lot of interest.

TRAFFIC DIRECTOR AND PARKING LOT. Upon arrival at the project, a security person would place a numbered cone on the hood of each visitor's vehicle and direct him or her to the sales area. A large sales force was available on weekends to accommodate the crowd. During the week, an off-site sales group was busy searching for potential buyers. Direct-mail marketing invited people to attend a dinner to hear about the wonderful community being constructed. If interested in touring the area, visitors were asked for a $5 deposit to be refunded upon arrival at the lake. This group of prospects was given a tour by one of the off-site salesmen. The on-site sales force toured the customers arriving during the weekdays.

SALES AREA AT THE ENTRANCE. Potential customers would see this scene upon their arrival on a weekend. Salesmen swarmed the area, making their customers as comfortable as possible in the middle of the construction process. The lake opened for sales at the end of March, and newspapers reported over a million dollars in sales. However, the formal opening occurred in mid-June 1968, and the public response was overwhelming.

POTENTIAL BUYERS ON TOUR. Pictured here are a salesman and his customers. He is rushing over to check with another salesman to see if the lot was sold. They would communicate by CB radio to the sales booth in the parking lot for the latest update on available lots. It was common to see several salesmen waiting to show the same lot, as over 75 salesmen were assigned to the project.

SALESMAN AND CLIENTS. This photograph of unidentified persons shows a typical sales scene. A salesman would drive his customer to a location, unroll his map, and try to explain exactly where a particular lot would be located. This procedure happened repeatedly while the roads and lots were still under construction. Some current residents of Canyon Lake still recall that hectic rush to purchase lots.

ANOTHER NEW ENTRANCE. Fred Hartman, one of the salesmen, stands beside the sign at the new entrance. Improvements began on the entrance, and the sign was moved into the median of a four-lane paved road before this photograph was taken. The area was beginning to seem more like a small community.

GATEHOUSE AND SALES PAVILION. This new gatehouse was located in the median strip of the road directly across from the sales pavilion. The small building in the bottom photograph was the control area for salesmen and radio communications. Customers were escorted to a building, instead of a table under an umbrella, to get further information or to sign papers. The larger building is now Bluebird Hall and is located on the corner of Canyon Lake Drive South and Bluebird Drive. This building once housed the mailboxes of the residents and later became a meeting place for various organizations, including the Canyon Lake Community Church.

CANYON VILLAGE STORE. Construction of a general store started in March 1968 at the same location the previous resort-office building was located. The store included a snack bar, covered porch, and restrooms, as well as a large interior room for general merchandise. The original ice-dispensing building from the previous resort was moved to the east side of the building. The Village Store, centrally located on Village Way, was near the amphitheater, marina, and launch ramp. It quickly became the focal point of the area, especially for the salesmen and their customers. The author and her husband managed the store four years for the Corona Land Company, and later Bruce and Marlene Lord leased the store and marina.

VILLAGE STORE INTERIOR.
The decor of the store was rustic, resembling an early-day mercantile in the countryside. Antiques and furnishings from Corona Foothill Lemon Company Store were displayed. A large, old-fashioned safe sat next to a showcase displaying artifacts from the Evans family. Above the showcase, a four-foot square plaque told the history of the area. A potbellied stove in the center of the room was a focal point, and a few chairs provided seats for visiting. Male clerks wore straw hats and garters on their sleeves to provide an authentic look. Store merchandise consisted of food staples, refrigerated items, old-fashioned candy sticks in glass jars, water skis and accessories, and other items visitors might need for the weekend.

VILLAGE STORE VERANDA. This photograph shows a part of the long veranda on the front of the building. Chairs surround tables made from whiskey barrels. Salesmen often brought their prospects here to give their sales pitch, treat them to refreshments, and send them off on a boat tour of the lake.

CANYON QUEEN TOUR BOAT. The pontoon boat shown here cruises around the lake, giving its riders a tour of the shoreline. Named the *Canyon Queen*, the boat gave potential buyers a different view of the lake than a land tour did. The driver was not a sales representative and only pointed out the different sights. After a few years, the boat was retired and moved to Lake Nacimiento, near Paso Robles.

CONSTRUCTION OF THE MARINA. Dredging and dirt removal for a private marina began in front of the parking lot at the Village Store. The ground was lowered about 20 feet from its existing elevation, and the docks would have spaces to moor 50 boats when finished. In later years, as the result of a lawsuit settlement, the marina closed and became a waterfront for several homes.

MARINA CONSTRUCTION COMPLETED. Shown in this photograph is the marina filling with water. The marina, located next to the Village Store, changed the shoreline in front of the store, and when docks, a walkway, and steps were installed, it would be available for property owners to rent boats or to moor their own.

MARTINS LANDING SIGN. The developers decided to name the marina Martins Landing and placed this nautical sign at the entrance to the boat dock. Four years later, the sign and business would be moved to Martin's Storage on Loch Lomond Drive, where it remained for 27 years.

FISHING BOATS FOR RENT. Donald Martin moved a few of his fishing boats to the marina, where they were made available for rent. A small building on the dock housed the outboard motors, oars, and life preservers. Many new property owners were previous customers of Railroad Canyon Lake Resort and continued to enjoy the good fishing.

71

TWO VIEWS OF THE MARINA. The top photograph shows the *Canyon Queen* moored at the dock and awaiting riders. During the weekdays, the activity was slow around the Village Store and marina, but on weekends, the place became crowded. The trees in the background on the right mark the campground of the previous resort. Campers continued to use this area until the permanent one on the west side of the lake was built. The bottom photograph, taken in 1968, shows the marina completed, landscaping finished, and the private docks in use. Across the lake the lodge is still under construction.

THE MAIN CAUSEWAY CONSTRUCTION. Construction started immediately on a 700-foot main causeway that would cross the lake near Village Way to Canyon Lake Drive North. The depth of the water on the north side was about 35 feet, and huge machines hauled and pushed dirt into the water for at least three weeks. Most of the fill dirt came from the area now known as the start of Canyon Lake Drive North and Clubhouse Drive. Hilltops were lowered, and the dirt used for fill on both sides of the causeway. The photograph at the bottom of the page shows the scarred hilltop near Village Way. The shoreline on the south side was not quite as deep as on the north side.

CONSTRUCTION OF A BOAT PASS. The 1969 spring issue of *Highway Urban Construction* stated, "Corona Land Company decided to purchase a 24-foot-diameter Armco Multi-Plate Pipe, 192 feet long, in five gage corrugated steel, with step-beveled ends. It was designed into the project by McCutchan and Associates of Pasadena, California to comply with Riverside County road specifications. Lacking a better name, the owners and residents of the community simply call it a 'boat pass,' although it is also an equalizer tube." The boat pass solved the problem for residents who once had to drive several miles around the lake to access the shopping areas and other amenities. In addition, two 12-foot-diameter vehicular underpasses were installed at the golf course. In the photograph below, workers tightening bolts in the plate stand on the scaffolding inside the tube.

CAUSEWAY BEFORE TUBE INSTALLATION. This photograph shows the causeway ready for the installation of the tube. This view, taken from the lodge area looking east, shows the road construction on Canyon Lake Drive North. The high mountain in the background is part of the area known as Canyon Lake Estates on Sorrel Lane.

CAUSEWAY AFTER TUBE INSTALLATION. This photograph, looking south from Canyon Lake Drive North, shows the causeway after the tube was installed, as well as the height of the roadway from the lake. The current roadway, now landscaped with trees and grass, gives a nice appearance to the community.

UNDERWATER-DIVING OPERATION. This professional diver works from the floating dock. The developer decided to remove the trees from the shoreline to make the lake appear larger. It worked; however, some fish habitat was destroyed in the process, and, in later years, the trees grew back again.

HELICOPTER SPREADING SEEDS. Wildflower seeds sown from this helicopter produced a beautiful scene in the spring. The sowing happened one time only, but the seeds mixed with native flowers and continued to grow for many years. Their growth slowly diminished as houses appeared but, if rains occur at the right time, the hills between Canyon Lake and Lake Elsinore come alive with wildflowers.

AMPHITHEATER NEAR THE VILLAGE STORE. The developers built this 300-seat amphitheater near the Village Store for the community to hold special events. Located next to the boat-launching ramp, the amphitheater only held one performance, by Mimi's School of Stars, a Norco dance club. A property owner arranged for the group to perform; unfortunately, the only photograph the author had was too dark to use, as it was taken during the performance that night. The photograph at the bottom of the page shows the area flooded in February 1969 and the author sitting in the boat. The amphitheater was later removed and became part of the swimming beach at Holiday Harbor.

ADVERTISING CARD AND NEWSPAPER INSERT. This artist's vision of the lake appeared on postcards and newspaper inserts. One insert read, "Here is the first private membership lake of its kind ever built in Southern California. Canyon Lake will be a private $45,000,000 water sports and recreation wonderland for just 5,000 families." It also mentioned choice lots on sale from $5,500 and such amenities as an 18-hole regulation golf course, equestrian area, tennis courts,

and a lodge. One page read, "Completed within 275 days! The lodge . . . swimming pool . . . tennis courts . . . the marina . . . the village center . . . beaches . . . park and campground site." The back page included a coupon to mail in for additional information or to receive a validated gate pass for a boat tour of the lake. It was compared with Lake Arrowhead and Lake Tahoe and advertised as only 90 minutes from Los Angeles.

LODGE UNDER CONSTRUCTION. Construction began on the two-story lodge when the causeway was almost finished. The 11,000-square-foot lodge, done in California ranch style, would be ready in time for the holidays. The upper floor would consist of a dining room, cocktail bar, and a large meeting room with a fireplace on the north end. Downstairs would be reserved for offices, a game room, restrooms, and showers for the pool and beach area.

AERIAL VIEW OF LODGE. This aerial view shows the finished lodge in the foreground and the Village Store and marina in the background. The water-treatment plant is located in the upper right, Martin's Storage facility and barn at the top of the hill, and the Martins' home just below. Corona Land Company used the previous trailer park for their construction, sales, and management offices.

CANYON LAKE LODGE. This photograph shows the west face of the lodge and the Z-shaped pool. The wraparound porch allowed entry in several places, and the dining room in the middle overlooked the lake and lighthouse. The multipurpose room on the left served as a meeting place and overflow dining room. The Property Owners Association offices occupied the lower floor, and originally one room served as a youth center.

THE LODGE BAR, 1968. Ann Holden, wife of general manager Frank Holden, stands behind the sunken horseshoe-shaped cocktail bar. The lodge opened in December 1968, just before Christmas, and soon became a focal point of the community. Frank Holden was in charge of all community functions and the golf course, which was under construction. The bar and dining room would be remodeled several times during the next 20 years.

FIRST LUAU AT THE LODGE. About 400 people attended this Hawaiian luau, and the price was $7.50 per person. This was the first of many successful events held at the lodge. Since no residences were under construction until late 1968, the property owners and their guests used the campground and lodge to get acquainted with their future neighbors.

CANYON VILLAGE NURSERY. The developer built a nursery in the summer of 1969 on the west side of the Village Store. Trees, shrubs, and a full line of supplies were available at wholesale prices to assist the property owners in beautifying their lots. The nursery also offered a regular maintenance-service program for absent homeowners.

CANYON LAKE LIGHTHOUSE.
These photographs show the lighthouse under construction and the finished product, complete with landscaping. The lodge and lighthouse construction happened simultaneously, and the low water level was a plus. Note the higher water level in the photograph below. The lighthouse was the idea of Gordon Heath, president of Corona Land Company, and is similar to the Nantucket lighthouse in Massachusetts. It was built on a one-third scale, and the base is 10 feet in diameter, tapering to seven feet at the deck level and rising 24 feet above the ground. The red-beacon light rotated and, at night, guided boaters to the campground or to the lodge.

ARTISTIC VIEW OF THE LIGHTHOUSE. This nautical landscaping built on a point of land between the lighthouse and the lodge offered an interesting view, as shown in this photograph. During construction, the low water level made it possible to walk from the lodge area to the lighthouse. Later the netting and poles were removed as the water rose and buoys were set to alert boaters to the shallow area.

RISING WATER AT THE LIGHTHOUSE, 1969. The winter rains in February 1969 raised the lake level rapidly and soon flowed over the dam. Since more water was arriving than leaving, parts of the causeways, beaches, parks, and the lighthouse were soon flooded. This photograph, taken February 24 at 2:00 p.m., shows the height of the waterline, and it continued to rise even higher the next day.

VIEW OF MARINA AND LIGHTHOUSE. The marina and Martins Landing appear in the foreground of this photograph, while the completed $550,000 lodge is visible in the middle. The lake level is low, and the lighthouse is still connected to the lodge area by a strip of land, so the date of this photograph would be 1968. Another short dock is seen on the left of the photograph.

ANOTHER VIEW OF THE LODGE. This photograph, taken when the lake level was high, shows the lodge area landscaped and the lighthouse surrounded by water. The house in the foreground, built by Foothill Construction Company, was one of their five model homes, ranging in price from $16,000 to $30,000. They built no more homes after these five and turned their attention to the Corona area.

FIRST GOLFING FOURSOME. Pictured here are, from left to right, Lee Hannah of Quail Valley, Steve Martin (caddy), Wayne Martin (caddy), Frank Holden (general manager of the lodge and golf course), Hubert Addy (lodge chef), and Dino Serafini of the Corona Land Company. Construction started on the course in October and was expected to be finished by the spring of 1969. However, the winter rains delayed the opening until later in the year. The photograph at the bottom of the page shows the course 37 years later, in 2006, as it undergoes an annual reseeding and maintenance program.

TWO VIEWS OF SAME LOCATION. Arthur and Frank Swanson lived in this house from about 1924 until their deaths. Frank was the last brother living and sold his property to the Corona Land Company with the stipulation he could live out the rest of his life on the property. He died shortly after Canyon Lake construction started. The tallest tree in the bottom photograph was the location of the Swanson house that was demolished by Corona Land Company. The current location is the No. 11 tee. Cottonwood Creek follows the edge of the golf course and flows through a concrete drainage ditch. According to the second golf professional at Canyon Lake, Phil Edmondson, as of February 1971, only two golfers had broken par and no one had managed a hole in one on the course.

PRACTICE PUTTING GREEN, 1969. Donald Martin practices on the putting green while the landscape crew work to beautify the grounds surrounding the clubhouse. Ted Robinson designed the course, and John Kile was the first golf professional. The course started at 6,400 yards and a par 71, however, the yardage was reduced through the years, but par remained at 71. This putting green is now the green for the No. 11 tee. The current clubhouse, pictured below, is now the Canyon Lake Country Club and is open to the public for food and beverage. The course, however, remains private.

GOLF CARTS FOR RENT. The golf carts stored under the porch are ready for renting. The course, designed by Ted Robinson, covered 135 acres on both sides of the highway and cost $500,000, according to the *Canyon Lake News*, a publication of the Corona Land Company. Green fees for 18 holes were advertised as $1.50 for property owners on weekdays and $3 on weekends. Guests of property owners paid $3 or $5, depending on the day of the week. The bottom photograph, taken from Early Round Drive, shows the course and clubhouse in the middle and Fairway Estates at the top. The Fairway Estates surround part of the golf course, and two passage tunnels under Railroad Canyon Road allow the golfers access to both sides.

OVERLOOKING THE GOLF-COURSE AREA. This photograph shows an overview of the golf course, clubhouse, and surrounding area. A home on Early Round Drive (far left) is visible, and others appear in the vicinity. The sycamore trees in the foreground were on the old Swanson property, and the pond is reclaimed water for irrigation of the golf course. A small lake appears on the left side of the clubhouse as well as its bank landscaped with rock and the name of the golf course. The men's golf club formed in 1971 with Ralph Brogdon elected president of the approximately 50 members. The club currently lists approximately 467 members. The women's golf club, formed in 1970, is approaching 200 members. The bottom photograph, taken in 1969 from the current No. 5 tee, shows the fairway going south to Railroad Canyon Road.

CURRENT SCENES OF THE GOLF COURSE. These unidentified golfers are finishing on the 11th green before crossing to the other side of the clubhouse to continue on to No. 12. Two- and three-story houses line the perimeter of the course, as shown in the top photograph. The terrain on the south side of Early Round Drive is extremely steep; however, the view of the countryside makes up for the lack of a backyard. The *Canyon Lake News* said there was an interesting hole on the course that was 135 yards away from the tee and 100 feet below to the green. That hole is now No. 15 and is 132 yards away from the tee.

NORTH CAUSEWAY CONSTRUCTION. Development on the western side of the lake depended on the construction of a bridge or causeway across the lake. Riverside County required all-weather access from the west side to other main roads, and Corona Land Company did not own the surrounding land. Leta Evans granted an easement that solved the problem, linking the project with a main road farther west. This entrance, known as the North Gate, saves residents time when they commute to work or go shopping. The top photograph shows the large steel tubes that allow water to flow back and forth under the road. They are the same type as the ones used in the main causeway, only smaller. The bottom photograph shows the causeway as it looks today.

EAST BAY VIEW. This photograph, taken in 1969 from the top of Sorrell Lane, shows a few houses built in the East Bay area. Dredging and extensive earth moving changed this flat farmland into building pads and small coves to accommodate more waterfront lots. Quail Valley appears in the top left of the photograph and the snowcapped San Bernardino Mountains on the right.

LOOKING WEST FROM SORRELL LANE. The highest point on Sorrell Lane provides a great view of Canyon Lake. This photograph, taken in 1969, looks west. The corner of the commercial area is seen on the left, and the trees at Indian Beach appear on the right. The Towne Center (current name) boasts a motel, restaurants, bank, real estate offices, and a variety of other businesses to accommodate the residents.

LOOKING NORTH FROM SORRELL LANE. This 1969 photograph, taken from Sorrell Lane, looks north, and the Indian Beach trees are on the left side. The barren flat area in the middle is between Cinnamon Teal, Emperor Drive, and Buck Tail Drive. The previous hilltop provided dirt for the realignment of Railroad Canyon Road.

INDIAN BEACH PARK AREA. Property owners and guests enjoyed all the parks, especially this one at Indian Beach, the site of the first Evans Fish Camp. This photograph shows the improvements that made for delightful summer outings. Visitors could arrive by boat or by car and enjoy the shade trees, sandy beach, and swimming area.

94

STOCKING THE LAKE WITH
CATFISH. Pictured here in the
tank are some of the 5,000
channel catfish that were being
stocked into the lake in the east
bay. This species of catfish can
grow to the weight of 20 pounds
or more. A special truck from the
local hatchery delivered the fish
and then released them into calm
waters, where they could adjust
to the new area. Another load
of 7,500 pounds was delivered
the next year in November
1970. The species of fish in the
lake include largemouth bass,
crappie, bluegill, perch, and
catfish. Naturally, there are carp
and other forage fish that travel
downstream when Colorado
River water is imported. One
truckload of trout was imported
from Whitewater Hatchery
in Cabazon, but they did not
survive long in the warm water.

DISPLAY OF LARGEMOUTH BASS. Pictured from left to right are Jack Phillips (sales manager), Donald Martin of Martins Landing, James Carter (real estate broker), and Mac Rosgen (salesman). Martin brought a catch of largemouth bass to the sales pavilion for some publicity photographs. In the background is a large display map of the Canyon Lake master plan.

GEORGE GRAHAM'S CATFISH. Pictured here with three large catfish is George Graham of Elsinore, caretaker of the dam for the Temescal Water Company. Guarding the dam, taking water measurements, and patrolling for trespassers were a few of his duties. His hobbies were fishing, hunting, and looking for fishing lures when the lake was low.

FLOODED CAUSEWAY, FEBRUARY 1969. Heavy rains started around February 22, 1969, and continued for several days. This photograph, taken at 9:30 a.m. on February 25, shows the flooded main causeway. A photograph taken the day before shows only half of the boat passage covered. Salt Creek and the San Jacinto River were flowing from bank to bank, and roads were becoming impassable.

SALT CREEK AT RAILROAD CANYON ROAD. Runoff water from Winchester, Sun City, and Menifee was backing up against Railroad Canyon Road and beginning to overflow. Eight hours later, the road washed out. In later years, the rains again damaged the road, swept several cars into the lake, and forced residents to use other routes during storms.

OVERFLOWING OF RAILROAD CANYON DAM. The huge rush of water coming into the lake quickly sent the water level up and over the dam. This photograph shows a close-up of the water going over the top of the dam. Water entered the lake faster than it could continue downstream to Lake Elsinore, causing the roads to be flooded.

PANORAMIC VIEW OF THE DAM. This photograph from February 26, 1969, shows another scene of water leaving the reservoir. The dam was transformed in 1998, when the walkway was removed and the sides cut back to allow water to flow over faster and avoid a lot of the flooding problems.

RAILROAD CANYON ROAD NEAR ELSINORE. The two-lane road leading to Elsinore often closed due to flooding. This photograph shows the last curve in the road before it reaches the current commercial area at Summerhill Drive. In earlier years, a single-person cable car stretched across the river at this point and provided a way to measure the water going down the river.

SAN JACINTO RIVER NEARING LAKE ELSINORE. Pictured here is the width of the river as it flows to Lake Elsinore. The water spreads out as it leaves the narrow canyon and continues downstream. Trees now line the riverbed for the entire route from the dam to the lake. The author remembers looking for crawfish in this area while her parents were shopping in town.

CANYON VILLAGE STORE PARKING LOT. This crowded parking lot at the Village Store overflowed with cars on Labor Day weekend in September 1968. Property owners brought their friends and relatives along to enjoy the lake and to introduce them to their salesman in hopes they, too, would buy property. Some salesmen gave property owners a finder's fee for referrals.

CAMPGROUND AT HOLIDAY HARBOR. Campers used the ledges of the previous campground to set up their tents and campers. This location is the current Holiday Harbor, and another type of smaller tree eventually replaced the ones in the background. The launch-ramp road is shown in the foreground.

OVERFLOW CAMPING AREA. This photograph, taken on the south side of the launch ramp, shows campers in the overflow area. Property owners and their guests could camp free of charge, but it was necessary to register first. Donald Martin was in charge of that detail. He was busy driving back and forth between the Village Store, campground, and the other overflow areas on that 1968 Labor Day weekend.

CAMPERS ACROSS FROM SKIPPERS ISLAND. Another overflow area across the lake from Skippers Island (shown in this photograph) accommodated more campers on Labor Day 1968. Construction of the roads and campground did not start on the west side of the lake until the following year. Campers continued to use several of the overflow areas on Memorial Day, Labor Day, and promotional weekends until 1970.

CAMPING AT SIERRA PARK. Camping was allowed in Sierra Park until the north causeway became a reality. After that, everyone used the campground that is now known as Happy Camp. Sierra Park developed into a beautiful park that people still enjoy today. Many property owners camped almost every weekend, and friendships formed that have lasted through the years.

NEW CAMPGROUND ON A WEEKEND. Property owners enjoyed this new campground, and waterfront spaces were always the first to be occupied. As of 2006, the camp has 76 spaces—36 with full hookups—and permanent managers Dwight and Peggy Cogdill live on the premises. A campground committee has formed and is looking forward to upgrading the area.

NEW CAMPGROUND OVERFLOW AREA. This photograph of Hidden Duck Cove and Strawberry Lane shows the area next to the campground before any homes were constructed. With the completion of the north causeway and Longhorn Drive, property owners used the new campground, and busy weekends found many using the adjacent land as an overflow area and enjoying the waterfront.

HOT-AIR BALLOON. The hot-air balloon pictured here is landing on White Sail Place, and the chase vehicle waits to assist in deflating and loading it into the truck. These balloons usually launched from the Perris Airport and were a remarkable sight. One house is visible on Vacation Drive, and Martin's Storage area can be seen at the top left of the photograph.

EQUESTRIAN-TRAINING ARENA. Looking north from the arena, the judge's stand is on the left, the barn in the back, and Longhorn Drive in the middle of the photograph. Advertising material from Corona Land Company mentions the 12-acre, $30,000 facility as having a training ring, barn, tack and feed room, and areas for boarding horses.

COMPLETED EQUESTRIAN AREA. This photograph shows the completed barn and the facility in use. *Canyon Lake News* mentions free board and room for a horse if the Property Owners Association can use it for renting. Patty and Jolene Holden, daughters of general manager Frank Holden, owned Canyon Queen One, the first colt born at the stables.

OLD AND NEW BARNS. These two photographs show the before and after views of the horse barns. The new barn bears the name of "William 'Billy' Fodor Jr." and includes a tack room for each stall. A total of 54 stalls and individual corrals rent from $160 to $245, including the cost of feed and cleaning. As of 2006, no horses were available for rent. An equestrian-center supervisor lives on the premises, and a trainer on staff gives riding lessons. The equestrian club has the responsibility of putting on different events, which include a monthly play day.

TRAIL RIDING ALONG THE LAKE. Horseback riders in this photograph enjoy a leisurely ride along the western shore of the main lake next to the current Catfish Cove. Homes would soon appear, and riding trails would soon change to the Bureau of Land Management property across from Treasure Island. The Village Store area and marina under construction are visible in the middle of this publicity shot.

EASTERN VIEW FROM LOCH LOMOND. In this view, looking northeast from the author's home, the snowcapped San Bernardino Mountains are visible. Canyon Lake streets are paved, homes have begun to appear, and small trees grow along the roadways. In the foreground, Loch Lomond Drive remains vacant, with no home construction at the time.

VIEW OF MAIN LAKE. This early view of the main lake, taken from the author's home on Loch Lomond Drive, shows the lodge building finished and homes on the west side of the lake. The previous trailer park-area can be seen in the foreground and later would become home sites with a panoramic view of the lake.

LATER VIEW OF MAIN LAKE. This photograph from the same location shows the lodge and homes along the west side of the lake. Homes now appear on both sides of Loch Lomond Drive, and the author's view of the lake is diminishing. Other than the resort area, a photograph from this same location before 1968 would show barren land and only a lone juniper tree in the distance.

WESTERN VIEW FROM LOCH LOMOND. An undeveloped island appears in the middle of this photograph looking northwest from the author's home. Current Catfish Cove is on the left and paved Longhorn Drive appears on the right of the island. The large eucalyptus trees on Village Way were still standing but would disappear in later years.

LATER WESTERN VIEW OF LOCH LOMOND. This photograph shows quite a change from the one above. Now homes built on the west side of the lake blend in with those of Tuscany Hills, but a fence separates the two, and the lake remains private. Cattle once roamed the hills, but now homes cover the area, and the wildlife is slowly disappearing.

22800 CANYON LAKE DRIVE NORTH. Jay and Pauline Keegan, avid water-skiers, discovered that Canyon Lake was the perfect place to retire and enjoy their sport. He was the first property owner elected president of the Property Owners Association. This was the first house built in 1968; they later sold it, and the new owners completely remodeled the exterior. The current owners, Ken and Joyce Dettling, are remodeling the interior.

22900 GRAY FOX DRIVE. Fred and Ann Barillaro's home, built in 1969, was the third house here. Fred owned Amber Realty and operated his business from an office on Canyon Lake Drive South, along with O'Brien and Cathro, building contractors. When the commercial area opened, he moved his business into the Towne Center as the first tenant, and changed the name of his business to Canyon Lake Realty. Stephen Sellers now owns the business.

VIEW OF SIERRA PARK. In this 1973 photograph, the park has grass and a sandy beach but no playground. This view of Sierra Park seen from Inspiration Point shows two homes on Vacation Drive. The one on the left adjoining the park is 29347 Vacation Drive and was built by the Larry Uebersetzig family in 1971. Their son Chad was the first baby born in Canyon Lake.

VIEW OF GRAY FOX DRIVE. This photograph, taken in 1973, shows Gray Fox Drive and a scattering of homes built across the lake. The house on the right belongs to Edward and Joy Nicholls, who built it in 1972 as a weekend retreat. The lot cost $13,500 in 1969, and today the only vacant lot on the street is next door to their house and is listed for sale at $994,900.

GOLF COURSE AND CALCUTTA DRIVE. This photograph shows the south end of Calcutta Drive and current No. 14 on the golf course. The A-frame house built by Foothill Construction Company at the end of Calcutta blends into the landscape, and it is hard to imagine that this area would have homes built along the fairway in later years.

CLOSE-UP AERIAL VIEW, 1971. Only a few homes can be seen in this 1971 photograph. Skippers Island appears on the left and the campground to its right. The Village Store area, Martins Landing, and the boat and trailer storage are in the middle. A close look at the right corner reveals the Fairway Estates across from the golf course clubhouse.

AERIAL VIEW, 1968. The photographer, looking east, took this aerial photograph in 1968 from high above the current Tuscany Hills. It shows Railroad Canyon Lake and the surrounding valleys. The snowcapped San Jacinto Mountains on the right and the San Bernardino Mountains on the left look down on valleys that would soon change forever. The lake is shown here before any construction started. Quail Valley is in the middle of the photograph and the Romoland area is just beyond. Railroad Canyon Road appears as a small ribbon on the right side of the photograph and the current Audie Murphy project just above it. The core of Sun City is the cluster of white in the middle, left of Newport Road. When viewed from above, the lake takes on the appearance of a dragon, the tail being on the north end and its head at the dam.

AERIAL VIEW, 1971. This photograph was taken from the same location as the one in 1968 and shows the construction around the lake. Dirt for the north causeway came from the hilltop, shown in the photograph as a nearby white oval. The hilltop sold as a five-acre parcel and later split into two parcels. Just above is a small lake in Quail Valley, which is dry most of the time. Building pads on the west side of the lake are ready, and the road to the campground has been completed. The commercial area and Fairway Estates have been finished; however, the estates on Sorrell Lane are still barren land. The valley behind the Fairway Estates is now the community of Canyon Hills. Newport Road splits the top part of the photograph, and Holland Road is on the right. In earlier years, they built the roads one mile apart on the section lines, and one could measure the mileage by the roads.

AERIAL VIEW, 1985. This photograph shows the same area as it looked 14 years later. Houses have been constructed all around the lake and in Quail Valley also. The Canyon Lake Community Church grounds appear in white along the road in the top right corner. Gault Field can be seen next to the equestrian center in the lower left corner of the photograph.

ANOTHER VIEW, LOOKING EAST. Comparing landmarks, this photograph appears to be earlier than the one above. Looking east from Tuscany Hills, Loch Lomond Drive appears in the foreground and Martins Landing just above. The small area in the lower right serves as a viewing area for the dam and is a busy place when the lake is overflowing.

114

FIRST TENNIS COURTS. Here players are enjoying the new courts, built between the lodge parking lot and the villas. The Property Owners Association installed lights for nighttime play and later built more courts. Looking across the lake, very few homes appear at the time of this photograph.

TREASURE ISLAND AREA. In 1970, Volume 1, No. 9 of the *Canyon Lake News* stated, Treasure Isle Bridge nears completion, "the two-lane bridge is 24 feet wide, with a span of 102 feet from abutment to abutment, with elevation of the bridge bed 13.97 feet." The dredger, pictured here in 1971, removes tons of dirt and rock, making the channel wider and deeper to allow boat passage under the bridge.

CONDOMINIUM CONSTRUCTION. The 1971 spring issue of the *Canyon Lake News* offered 26 premium lots for sale on the four-acre island. "These exclusive condominium lots will range in price from $15,000 to $25,000 according to D.E. Serafini, president of Corona Land Company, and each will have its own boat slip."

TREASURE ISLAND BRIDGE, 2006. This photograph shows the bridge as it looks today. Since the island lots did not sell, and no one offered to purchase the entire island for $500,000, in 1973, the Corona Land Company decided to build 11 two-story units with four condominiums each, as pictured above. During the summer of 2006, several two-bedroom units sold for $500,000.

MARTINS LANDING STORAGE AREA. The Martins owned 45 acres adjacent to the community, and Gordon Heath asked if they wanted to open a boat-and-trailer storage facility for the property owners. Permits from the county were obtained, and the facility opened and continues today. The Martins retired in 1999, and the property today is known as Summerwood Landing and offers enclosed storage for boats and recreational vehicles.

NORTH VIEW OF STORAGE AREA. This view of Martins Landing shows the trailer houses parked in neat rows. A repair shop occupies the building in the middle of the photograph. Summer usually finds most of the 350 spaces occupied, but not as many boaters use the lake in the winter. Motor homes did not appear on the scene until later, as evidenced in this photograph taken in 1974.

EARLY CHURCH SERVICE. Shown in this photograph is one of the early church services held on the property at Sorrell Lane and Railroad Canyon Road. The large cross donated by Paul and Helen Mickel is still a landmark in front of the church. In 1973, Rae and Janet Simonson thought the community needed a church, others agreed, and a small group of families started to explore the idea.

CHURCH BUILDING PAD. Before obtaining this church property, the families would meet at the lodge on Sunday afternoons and visiting pastors from various denominations would fill the pulpit. Corona Land Company originally set aside several lots on Sorrell Lane for churches, but no religious groups responded. When approached by the small group, the company agreed to donate a parcel if the group would organize and incorporate as a community church.

118

CANYON LAKE COMMUNITY CHURCH CONSTRUCTION. Through a local pastor, the group was introduced to the Reformed Churches in America, and a summer student pastor arrived in 1975. The services moved from the lodge to the original sales pavilion (now Bluebird Hall). With the assistance of Rev. Chester Droog, the organizers voted to affiliate with the Reformed Churches in America. During this organizational period, a church-building fund was started, and donations began to arrive.

AFTER-CHURCH SOCIAL. Church members would meet after the service, enjoy refreshments, and share their enthusiasm about the new building under construction. Pictured here around the table are, from left to right, Ione Hyde, Helen Harter, Ruthe Lee, Paul Scott, and Alice Haddad (serving punch). A large ravine separated the church pad and the parking lot and was eventually filled with massive amounts of dirt.

CANYON LAKE COMMUNITY CHURCH. A building committee formed, with Donald Martin as the chairman. When donations reached $15,000, the decision was made to start the building. Groundbreaking took place on January 31, 1976, and construction progressed rapidly during the next 11 months as volunteers came forward to offer their services; donations seemed to match the needs in every phase of construction. "We just can't believe it," became the regular comment among the community members. Furnishings arrived from a variety of places, and to those involved, it became apparent that "Someone Great" was leading and guiding many, many hearts. One Sunday in October 1976, Pastor Peter Van Dyke, who was visiting from Illinois, preached the sermon before the church was completed. He returned in January 1977 as the first full-time pastor and continues to serve the community today.

NEW CHURCH BUILDINGS. The congregation grew, families with small children began attending services, and soon Canyon Lake Community Church needed to expand. After an adjacent parcel of land was purchased, construction began in April 1981 on another building, which would include a large multipurpose room and gym surrounded by classrooms and a kitchen. This large room became the center for church activities as the congregation continued to grow. Sunday services eventually outgrew the second building, and in December 1992, the current sanctuary was built. It now serves a membership of 950 with two services and a staff of 17. The original charter members numbered 102 in 1976, and some of them are still in attendance today. The first church is now the chapel and is used for small weddings and funerals.

CLOSE-UP VIEW, 1985. This aerial photograph, taken in 1985, shows Martins Landing storage area in the foreground and the surrounding streets. The vacant land still belongs to the Martins, and more homes have begun to appear along the surrounding streets. The Village Store and marina are still here, and the Holiday Harbor area is not yet developed.

ANOTHER AERIAL VIEW, 1985. This photograph, taken at the same time as the one above, shows an aerial view looking north toward Perris. The trees below the dam and along Cottonwood Creek can be seen in the lower part of the photograph. More waterfront homes have begun to appear, and the vacant lots are becoming fewer and fewer.

ELINOR'S RESTAURANT, 1990. The lodge restaurant, remodeled in 1990, held a contest to find a name for the new dining room. The winning entry was "Elinor's," after the author, the first lady to reside in Canyon Lake. Pictured here are the author and her husband, Donald, next to the sign. The restaurant carried the name for 10 years until a new lodge replaced the old one, and the name was changed to "the Lighthouse."

EVANS PARK SIGN. Evans Park West was one of nine parks shown on the original master plan but was never developed until 1987, when the Homeowners Club took on the project. Completed in 1990, the 1.8-acre park located on Canyon Lake Drive North is a par course with 12 stations and a one-quarter mile trail for jogging and walking. It is a tribute to the Evans family, pioneers of the area.

CORE SAMPLE FROM THE DAM. After the Baldwin Hills dam collapsed in 1963, the state ordered all dams inspected and reinforced. The project entailed cutting six-inch core samples of solid concrete almost 50 feet deep beneath the dam and 29 steel cables, encased in concrete, poured into each hole adding extra strength. The concrete found in the cores was stronger than current requirements in 1965. The total cost of the project was $80,000.

RAILROAD CANYON DAM MODIFICATION. Railroad Canyon dam underwent an extensive $9.1 million modification in 1996 to alleviate the flooding problems of recent years and to prepare for any future earthquakes or floods. The removal of the walkway over the spillway and the cutting back of the sides increased the spillway width from 193 feet to 376 feet.

WATER-TREATMENT PLANT. The photograph above shows the water-treatment plant next to the dam and the construction site during the modification of the dam in 1996. One of the roads in Tuscany Hills is visible, and houses would soon appear on the hills. The lower scene shows water going over the spillway on February 8, 1998. With a wider spillway, water can flow out faster than before and the amount of time the causeways need to close due to flooding has been lessened. However, the amount of water coming from the San Jacinto River and Salt Creek continues to increase each year as bare land is turned into housing developments. Elsinore Valley Municipal Water District purchased the Temescal Water Company in 1989 and now is the owner of the dam and lake.

CANYON LAKE PROPERTY OWNERS ASSOCIATION OFFICE. The current Canyon Lake Property Owners Association office is located in the Towne Center, across from the main gate. Property owners pay an annual assessment to provide the income to manage the private community, which is also a city. An elected board of directors is the governing body, and they hire a general manager to oversee the day-to-day operations.

CANYON LAKE CITY HALL. Canyon Lake incorporated as a city December 1, 1990, and their office is located in the Towne Center, adjacent to the Property Owners Association offices. The city council is the governing body of the City of Canyon Lake. City clerk Kathy Bennett has held her position since the city's incorporation.

THE AUTHOR, THEN AND NOW. This 1939 photograph shows the author feeding the geese at the first fish camp location, now known as Indian Beach. The lower photograph shows her sitting on the front patio of her home overlooking Canyon Lake. It has been quite a change going from the carefree days of being a child with no neighbors to being an adult living in a city of 10,000 residents.

Printed in the USA
CPSIA information can be obtained
at www.ICGtesting.com
LVHW080057211123
764443LV00008B/165